The Common Sense Guide to Investing

A Little Book of Simple and Effective Strategies

Chad K. Upshaw

Table of Contents

INTRODUCTION

Investing is one of the most essential and rewarding life skills to acquire. It may assist you in reaching your financial objectives, including saving for retirement, purchasing a home, or funding your children's school. It may also provide you with a feeling of fulfillment, stability, and independence.

Investing, on the other hand, maybe perplexing, daunting, and overwhelming. There are several alternatives, phrases, and techniques to consider. There are also other hazards, uncertainties, and emotions to consider. How do you decide what to do, when to do it, and why?

This is where this book comes into play. This book is intended to help you grasp the fundamentals of investing and use common sense concepts and tactics that have shown to be effective over time. This book is not about becoming wealthy quickly, winning the market, or forecasting the future. This book is about utilizing easy and practical strategies to regularly and securely develop your money.

The premise of this book is that investing is not rocket science, but rather common sense. The capacity to think sensibly, logically, and realistically is referred to as common sense. The capacity to avoid unneeded complexities, expenditures, and blunders is referred to as common sense. The capacity to learn from the experience and knowledge of others is referred to as common sense.

This book will teach you:

- ❖ The fundamentals of investing, such as what stocks, bonds, mutual funds, ETFs, risk, return, diversification, and so on are.

- ❖ Common sense investing practices, such as investing for the long term, avoiding fees and taxes, selecting low-cost index funds, rebalancing your portfolio, and so on.

❖ Common sense investment tactics, such as how to manage assets, adjust risk, prepare for alternative eventualities, and so on.

❖ The common sense investing dangers, such as how to prevent market timing, chasing profits, overconfidence, loss aversion, and so on.

❖ Common sense investment resources, such as how to locate and utilize trustworthy and valuable sources of knowledge and guidance, such as books, websites, podcasts, newsletters, and so on.

You will have a clear and confident grasp of how to invest with common sense by the conclusion of this book. You will be able to make wise and educated judgments based on your objectives, personality, and circumstances. You will be able to reap the advantages and rewards of investing without worry and inconvenience.

This book is not intended to be a complete or final investment guidance. It is intended to be a straightforward and effective investment guidance. It is intended to be a little book of common sense that you can quickly read, grasp, and use.

I hope you find this book useful and entertaining. I hope it motivates you to begin or better your investment path. I hope it will assist you in achieving your financial goals and living a happy and satisfying life. Thank you for taking the time to read this. Let's get started.

CHAPTER 1: INVESTING FUNDAMENTALS

Before delving into the common sense ideas and tactics of investment, we must first comprehend the fundamentals of investing. What exactly is investing? Why should you invest? How do you make investments? What are the different kinds of investments? What are the advantages and disadvantages of investing? These are some of the questions addressed in this chapter.

What exactly is investing?

Making your money work for you is the act of investing. It entails investing your money in assets that may create income or appreciate over time. Investing is distinct from saving, which involves storing your money in a secure location, such as a bank account, where it yields little or no return. Saving is useful for short-term objectives like purchasing a vehicle or taking a trip, but it is insufficient for long-term goals like retiring or paying for your children's school. Saving will not help you expand your wealth or combat inflation, which is the gradual increase in the cost of goods and services.

Investing, on the other hand, may assist you in achieving your long-term objectives by making your money work harder and smarter for you. Investing may help you increase your wealth by generating interest, dividends, or capital gains. Investing may also help you combat inflation by improving your money's buying power over time. Investing may also assist you in generating passive income, which is money earned without working, such as rent, royalties, or dividends. Passive income may provide you with greater financial independence and stability since it does not rely on your active income, which is money earned by working, such as salary, wages, or commissions.

However, investment is not a quick-fix solution that will make you wealthy overnight. Investing needs perseverance, dedication, and knowledge. Investing also entails risk or the danger of losing part or all of your money. Investing is not a one-size-fits-all answer since each individual has unique objectives, tastes, and circumstances. As a result, you must grasp the fundamentals of investing and how to apply them to your situation.

Why should you invest?

There are several reasons to invest, however, the following are the most important:

1. To accomplish your financial objectives: Investing may assist you in achieving your financial objectives, such as purchasing a home, establishing a company, or retiring comfortably. Investing allows you to make your money grow quicker and attain your objectives sooner than just saving. For example, if you save $100 per month for 30 years in a bank account paying 1% interest each year, you will have $41,851. However, if you invest the same amount every month for a year in a diverse portfolio earning 7% interest, you would finish up with $121,997. That's a $80,146 difference, or almost three times more!

2. To combat inflation: Investing may assist you in beating inflation, which is the gradual increase in the cost of goods and services. Inflation diminishes your money's buying power, which means you can purchase less with the same amount of money over time. For example, if the annual rate of inflation is 3%, a loaf of bread that costs $1 today will cost $1.03 next year, $1.06 the next year, and so on. The identical loaf of bread will cost $2.43, or more than double, in 30 years! If you leave your money in a bank account that pays 1% interest each year, it will lose value over time since the interest rate is lower than the rate of inflation. However, if you invest in a diverse portfolio that yields 7% interest each year, your money will grow in value over time since the interest rate is larger than the inflation rate.

3. To generate passive income: Investing may assist you in generating passive income, which is money earned without working, such as rent, royalties, or dividends. Passive income may provide you with greater financial independence and stability since it does not rely on your active income, which is

money earned by working, such as salary, wages, or commissions. Passive income may also assist you in achieving financial independence, which is defined as having enough money to pay for your living needs without working. For example, if you need $40,000 per year in living expenditures and have a diverse portfolio that yields 4% dividends per year, you will require $1,000,000 in your portfolio to create enough passive income to meet your expenses. That means you may retire or follow your interests without having to worry about money.

How do you make investments?

Investing is not as difficult as it may seem. To begin investing, you do not need to be a financial expert or have a lot of money. You only need to follow these basic steps:

> Establish your objectives: The first step in investing is to establish your objectives. What is the purpose of your investment? How much cash do you require? When will

you need it? How much danger are you willing to take? These are some of the questions you should consider before investing. Your objectives will help you decide how much to invest, where to invest, and for how long. For example, if you are saving for retirement, you may need a significant sum of money yet have a lengthy time horizon, allowing you to accept greater risk and invest in equities. However, if you are investing for a trip, you may only require a small amount of money and have a limited time horizon, so you should take less risk and invest in bonds or cash.

➢ Select your account: The next step in investing is to choose an account. What will you do with your money? You may invest in a variety of accounts, including brokerage accounts, retirement accounts, and education accounts. Each sort of account has its own set of benefits and drawbacks, such as fees, taxes, and limitations. You must choose the account that best meets your objectives and circumstances. If you are saving for retirement, for example, you may choose to utilize a retirement account, such as a 401(k) or an IRA, which provide tax advantages and incentives. However, if you are saving for school, you should choose a 529 plan or a Coverdell ESA, which both provide tax advantages and incentives.

➤ Select your investments: The last stage in investing is to select your investments. What are you going to purchase with your money? There are several investment options available, including stocks, bonds, mutual funds, ETFs, real estate, and commodities. Return, risk, liquidity, and diversity are all characteristics of different types of investments. You must choose assets that are appropriate for your objectives and risk tolerance. For example, if you desire big profits and can manage high risk, you can consider investing in stocks. If you desire modest returns and little risk, you might consider investing in bonds or cash.

What are the different kinds of investments?

There are several sorts of investments available, but the following are the most common:

> Stocks: Stocks are ownership shares in a firm. When you purchase a stock, you become a part-owner of the business and have the right to receive a percentage of the company's income, known as dividends, as well as vote on critical issues, such as the election of the board of directors. Stocks are often referred to as equities or shares. Stocks are regarded as the most dangerous, but also the most lucrative, sort of investment, since they may provide both enormous profits and severe losses. Stocks are also quite volatile, which means that their prices may fluctuate quickly and unexpectedly. Stocks are appropriate for long-term investors with a high-risk tolerance and a drive for growth.

➢ Bonds: Bonds are loans made to the government, corporations, or other entities. When you purchase a bond, you are lending money to the issuer in exchange for a predetermined amount of interest, known as the coupon, and the principal, or the initial amount of money, at a specified date known as the maturity. Bonds are sometimes known as debt securities or fixed-income securities. Bonds are seen to be less hazardous, but also less lucrative, than stocks since they provide lower returns while also having smaller losses. Bond prices are also less volatile than stock prices, implying that they are more stable and predictable. Bonds are appropriate for investors with a short to medium time horizon, a low to moderate risk tolerance, and an income need.

➢ Mutual funds: Mutual funds are groupings of stocks, bonds, or other assets professionally managed by a fund manager. When you purchase a mutual fund, you are purchasing a share of the fund and owning a piece of the securities in the fund. Mutual funds are also referred to as pooled investments or diversified investments. Mutual funds are seen to be a convenient and cost-effective method to invest because they provide diversification (spreading your money across several kinds of assets to lessen risk) and professional management (having an expert choose and monitor the securities for you). Mutual funds are appropriate for investors with a medium to long investment horizon, a moderate risk tolerance, and a desire for simplicity.

➢ ETFs: Similar to mutual funds, ETFs trade like stocks. ETFs are stock, bond, or other security portfolios that follow an index, such as the S& P 500, a sector, such as technology, or a theme, such as environmental, social, and governance (ESG). When you purchase an ETF, you are purchasing a share of the ETF and thereby owning a piece of the securities in the ETF. ETFs are also known as index funds or exchange-traded funds. ETFs are regarded as a flexible and effective investment vehicle since they provide diversity, low cost, and transparency. ETFs are appropriate for investors who wish to track a certain market, industry, or topic and value flexibility and efficiency.

These are the most common sorts of investments, but there are others, like as real estate, commodities, cryptocurrencies, and alternative investments, that you may investigate and learn more about. Each sort of investment has benefits and drawbacks that you should be aware of before investing.

What are the advantages and disadvantages of investing?

Investing has numerous advantages, but it also has many disadvantages. Investing has the following advantages:

- Growth: Investing may help you build money over time by generating interest, dividends, or capital gains. The rise in the value of your assets over time is referred to as growth. Growth may help you meet your financial objectives while beating inflation.

- Income: By receiving regular payments from your assets, such as interest, dividends, or rent, investing may assist you in generating passive income. Income is the money you get from your investments without having to work. Income may augment your active income and assist you in achieving financial independence and stability.

- Diversification: Investing may help you avoid risk by distributing your money across many forms of assets, such as stocks, bonds, or mutual funds. Diversification is the technique of having a diverse portfolio of assets that do not all move in the same direction at the same time. Diversification may help you reduce volatility while also protecting your portfolio from losses.

The following are the hazards of investing:

- Loss: Investing puts you at risk of losing part or all of your money. Loss is the gradual decline in the value of your assets. Losses may occur as a result of a variety of events, including market swings, economic downturns, firm failures, fraud, or human mistakes. Loss may have an impact on both your financial and emotional well-being.

- Volatility: Investing exposes you to the volatility and instability of your investments. Volatility is a measure of how much and how often the value of your assets changes over time. Volatility may be triggered by a variety of causes, including supply and demand, news, events, or emotions. Volatility may cause investors worry and anxiety, leading them to make illogical judgments.

- Liquidity: Investing might make it tough to turn your capital into cash. The simplicity and quickness with which you may sell your assets without altering their price is referred to as liquidity. Liquidity varies according to the kind of investment, market circumstances, and demand and supply. Liquidity may impact your capacity to access your money when you need it and to capitalize on opportunities or respond to crises.

These are the fundamentals of investing that you should understand before you begin investing. Investing may be a fun and profitable pastime, but it also demands patience, dedication, and expertise. In the next chapter, we will go over several common sense investing ideas that may help you invest intelligently and profitably.

CHAPTER 2: COMMON SENSE INVESTING PRINCIPLES

In the last chapter, we covered the fundamentals of investing, such as what investing is, why you should invest, how to invest, and what the many sorts of investments are. We will discover the common sense principles of investing in this chapter, which are the essential rules and recommendations that may help you invest intelligently and profitably.

These ideas are founded on the knowledge and experience of some of history's greatest successful investors, including Warren Buffett, Benjamin Graham, John Bogle, and Peter Lynch. Academic research and empirical facts back up these notions. These ideas are not difficult or obscure, but rather straightforward and obvious. They exemplify common sense investment.

The following are some common sense investment principles:

1. Invest for the long term: The first common sense investing guideline is to invest for the long term. This implies that when you invest, you should have a time horizon of at least five years, ideally 10 years or more. This also implies that you should avoid attempting to time the market, which is the effort to forecast future market moves and purchase or sell appropriately. Long-term investing offers several benefits, including:

   a. better returns: investment over the long term might help you obtain better returns than short-term investment. This is because the longer you invest, the more you may profit from compounding, which is the process of earning interest on your interest. Compounding may significantly increase your wealth over time. For example, if you invest $10,000 in a diverse portfolio that yields 7% interest each year, you would have $19,671 after ten years, $38,696 after twenty years, and $76,123 after thirty years. That's a $56,123 difference or more than five times more!

b. Lower risk: investment over the long term might help you lower your risk more than short-term investment. This is because the longer you invest, the more you can level out the market's inevitable and unexpected volatility. The market goes through ups and downs, but in the long run, it tends to go up more than down. For example, the S&P 500, an index of 500 significant US corporations, has generated positive returns in 73% of the years since 1926, and negative returns in just 27% of the years. However, while looking at the monthly performance, you will see that it has had good returns in 59% of the months and negative returns in 41% of the months. As a result, by investing for the long term, you may boost your chances of earning good market returns while avoiding negative market returns.

c. Lower costs: Investing in the long run might help you save money over the near term. This is because the less you trade, the less money you spend on fees, commissions, and taxes. These expenses may eat into your profits and erode your worth over time. For example, if you invest $10,000 in a diversified portfolio earning 7% interest per year and paying 1% in fees each year, you would have $16,367 in ten years, $26,765 in twenty years, and $43,865 in thirty years. However, if you pay 2% in fees and commissions every year, you will have $14,802 in ten years, $21,911 in twenty years, and $32,422 in thirty years. That's a $11,443 difference, or more than 25% less!

2. Avoid fees and taxes: The second common sense investing guideline is to avoid costs and taxes. This implies you should pay as little as possible to others for investing your money, such as brokers, fund managers, consultants, or the government. Fees and taxes are the enemies of investment since they erode profits and wealth over time. For example, if you invest $10,000 in a diversified portfolio that generates 7% interest per year while paying 1% in fees and commissions and 15% in taxes, you would have $13,513 in 10 years, $18,263 in 20 years, and $24,722 in 30 years. However, if you pay no fees or commissions and

no taxes, you will have $19,671 in 10 years, $38,696 in 20 years, and $76,123 in 30 years. That's a $51,401 difference, or more than twice!

How can you avoid paying fees and taxes? Here are some pointers:

❖ Select low-cost investments: The first recommendation for avoiding fees and taxes is to select low-cost assets, such as index funds or exchange-traded funds (ETFs) that have minimal or no fees and commissions. Index funds and exchange-traded funds (ETFs) are pools of stocks, bonds, or other assets that reflect an index, such as the S& P 500, a sector, such as technology, or a theme, such as environmental, social, and governance (ESG). Index funds and ETFs provide diversity, low cost, and transparency by attempting to equal the performance of the index, sector, or theme that they track rather than beating it. In comparison to actively managed funds, which are collections of stocks, bonds, or other securities that are selected and monitored by a fund manager who tries to beat the market using various strategies such as research, analysis, or timing, index funds, and ETFs typically charge less than 0.5% in fees and commissions per year. Actively managed funds often underperform the market after fees and taxes and generally charge more than 1% in fees every year. As a consequence, by selecting low-cost investments like index funds or ETFs, you may save money while achieving superior performance.

❖ Select tax-efficient investments: The second advice for avoiding fees and taxes is to select tax-efficient assets, such as stocks, bonds, or mutual funds, which produce little or no tax. Taxes differ based on the kind of investment, type of income, and type of account. In general, you may receive three sorts of income from your investments: interest, dividends, and capital gains. Interest is money earned by lending your money, such as bonds or bank accounts. Dividends are payments made to you as a result of holding a share of a corporation, such as stocks or mutual funds. Capital gains are the profits you get when you sell your assets for a higher price than you purchased them, such as stocks or mutual funds. Depending on your tax rate, holding term, and account type, each source of income is taxed differently. Interest is generally taxed at your regular income tax rate, which may vary between 10% and 37% depending on your income level.

Dividends may be taxed at your regular income tax rate or a reduced rate of 0%, 15%, or 20%, depending on your income level and whether or not the dividends are eligible. Qualified dividends are dividends that meet certain criteria, such as being paid by a US corporation or a foreign corporation eligible for a tax treaty with the US, and being held for more than 60 days within 121 days surrounding the ex-dividend date, which determines who is entitled to the dividend. Depending on your income level and whether the capital gains are short-term or long-term, capital gains may be taxed at your regular income tax rate or a reduced rate of 0%, 15%, or 20%. Short-term capital gains are profits made from selling assets within a year after purchasing them. Long-term capital gains are capital gains generated when you sell your assets after a year of ownership. As a result, by selecting tax-efficient assets, such as stocks, bonds, or mutual funds, you may save money and retain more of your earnings.

❖ Select tax-advantaged accounts: The third advice for avoiding fees and taxes is to select tax-advantaged accounts that give tax advantages and incentives, such as retirement accounts or school accounts. You may invest in a variety of accounts, including brokerage accounts, retirement accounts, and education accounts. Each sort of account has its own set of benefits and drawbacks, such as fees, taxes, and limitations. Brokerage accounts, in general, are the most flexible and accessible, but also the least tax-efficient, since they provide no tax advantages or incentives. Every year, regardless of whether you withdraw your money or not, you must pay taxes on your income and capital gains. Retirement accounts are the most tax-efficient, but also the least flexible and accessible, since they provide tax advantages and incentives while imposing limits and penalties.

Traditional and Roth retirement accounts are the two basic categories. Traditional retirement plans, such as a 401(k) or an IRA, enable you to deduct your contributions from your taxable income, which means you pay less taxes now, but you must pay taxes on withdrawals at your regular income tax rate later. Roth retirement accounts, such as a Roth 401(k) or a Roth IRA, do not enable you to deduct your contributions from your taxable income, which means you pay taxes now but do not have to pay taxes later if you follow the regulations. The rules for retirement accounts require you to begin withdrawing your money at a certain age, known as the required minimum distribution (RMD) age, which is 72 for most people, and to pay a 10% penalty if you withdraw your money before that age, known as the early withdrawal age, which is 59 and a half for most people unless you qualify for an exception, such as disability, education, or medical expenses.

Education accounts are the most particular and focused, but they are also the most stringent and limiting since they provide tax advantages and incentives while simultaneously imposing regulations and constraints. 529 plans and Coverdell ESAs are the two basic forms of education accounts. 529 plans are government-sponsored programs that enable you to save money for eligible school expenditures like tuition, fees, books, or room and board for yourself or a beneficiary like a child or grandchild. Coverdell ESAs are federal programs that enable you to save money for eligible education expenditures such as private school tuition, uniforms, or transportation for a beneficiary under the age of 18. The tax advantages and incentives for education accounts include the fact that you do not have to pay taxes on your profits as long as you use them for qualifying school costs, and you may be eligible for state tax deductions or credits, depending on your state and plan.

The rules and limitations for education accounts are that there is a maximum annual contribution limit of $15,000 for 529 plans and $2,000 for Coverdell ESAs and that you may face taxes and penalties if you use your money for non-qualified expenses or change your beneficiary to someone who is not a family member. As a result, by selecting tax-advantaged accounts, such as retirement or school accounts, you may save money while also receiving tax advantages and incentives.

3. Select quality investments: The third common sense investing guideline is to select quality investments. This implies you should invest in firms or securities with solid fundamentals such as profits, growth, cash flow, assets, competitive advantage, innovation, or sustainability. Quality investments are more likely to outperform the market over time and to endure downturns and shocks. Quality investments are also more likely to provide dividends, which are recurring payments made by a corporation for holding a portion of its stock. Dividends may offer income while also increasing your profits over time.

How do you choose high-quality investments? Here are some pointers:

- Search for earnings: The first advice for selecting great investments is to search for earnings, which are the profits generated by a company's activities. Earnings are a company's primary source of value and growth because they indicate its capacity to create cash and reinvest it in its operations. Earnings are also the primary driver of stock prices since they represent a company's prospects and possibilities.

By looking at earnings, you may locate lucrative organizations, expanding, and appealing. profits per share (EPS), which is profits divided by the number of shares outstanding, and earnings growth, which is the percentage change in earnings from one period to the next, are two ways to quantify a company's earnings. You may also compare a company's profits to those of its peers, industry, or market to see how it compares. For example, if you want to invest in a technology firm, search for one with a high EPS, strong earnings growth, and high earnings compared to its rivals, sector, or the S& P 500.

- Seek for value: The second advice for selecting great investments is to seek value, which is the difference between an investment's price and its worth. The term "value" refers to how inexpensive or costly an investment is in comparison to its fundamentals, which include profits, growth, cash flow, assets, and dividends. Value is also a measure of how much you pay for what you receive, as well as how much you get for what you pay for.

By searching for value, you may uncover undervalued assets, meaning they are worth more than they cost, and that provide a margin of safety, defined as the gap between the price and the inherent value of an investment. Various ratios, such as price-to-earnings (P/E), which is the price divided by earnings, or dividend yield, which is the dividend divided by the price, may be used to determine the value of an investment. You may also compare the value of an investment to that of its peers, industry, or market to evaluate how it is valued in comparison to others. For example, if you want to buy in a utility business, search for one with a low P/E ratio, a high dividend yield, and a cheap valuation in comparison to its rivals, its industry, or the S& P 500.

- Check for potential: The third guideline for selecting great investments is to check for potential, which is the possibility or chance that an investment's value or performance may rise in the future. Potential measures how much space or opportunity an investment has to expand, develop, or innovate, as well as how much risk or uncertainty it confronts to accomplish its objectives. Potential also denotes how much an investment may profit from trends, changes, or advancements in its industry, market, or environment. By looking for potential, you can find investments with a competitive advantage, which is an investment's ability to outperform its rivals or the market, and a sustainable advantage, which is an investment's ability to maintain or increase its competitive advantage over time. You can assess an investment's potential by using various indicators, such as growth rate, which is the percentage change in a fundamental factor, such as earnings, sales, or assets, from one period to the next, or innovation rate, which is the percentage of revenue or profit generated by new products, services, or markets.

You may also compare an investment's potential to that of its peers, industry, or market to see how it compares to others. For example, if you want to invest in a consumer products firm, search for one with a high growth rate, a high rate of innovation, and a high potential in comparison to its rivals, its industry, or the S&P 500.

4. Diversify your portfolio: The fourth common sense investing guideline is to diversify your portfolio. This indicates that you should diversify your

investments, such as stocks, bonds, or cash, as well as across sectors, industries, geographies, or topics. Diversification may aid in risk reduction since various investments may respond differently to the same market circumstances or occurrences. Diversification may also help you enhance your profits since various investments might provide you with different chances or benefits. Diversification is the practice of spreading your eggs over several baskets rather than placing all of your eggs in one basket.

How can you broaden your portfolio? Here are some pointers:

a. Diversify across asset classes: The first advice for diversifying your portfolio is to diversify between asset classes, which are broad investment categories such as stocks, bonds, or cash. Return, risk, liquidity, and diversity are all features of each asset type. Stocks, in general, provide bigger rewards but also more risk than bonds or cash. Bonds provide lesser yields while simultaneously being less risky than stocks or cash. Cash provides lower returns, but also lower risk and more liquidity than equities or bonds. As a result of diversifying among asset classes, you can manage risk and return while still having access to your money when you need it. As we mentioned in the previous chapter, you may determine your asset allocation, which is the proportion of your portfolio that you invest in each asset class, depending on your objectives, preferences, and circumstances.

For example, if you are saving for retirement and have a long time horizon, a high-risk tolerance, and a desire for growth, you may wish to invest 70% in stocks, 20% in bonds, and 10% in cash. However, if you are investing for a trip and have a short time horizon, a low-risk tolerance, and a need for income, you may choose to put more in bonds or cash, say 50% and 40%, and less in equities, say 10%.

b. Diversify within asset classes: The second recommendation for diversifying your portfolio is to diversify within asset classes, which are investment divisions like kinds, sectors, industries, geographies, or themes. Return, risk, liquidity, and diversity are all features of each subcategory. There are numerous categories of stocks, such as large-cap, mid-cap, or small-cap, which relate to the company's size, or value, growth, or mix, which refers to the company's style.

Bonds may also be classified as government, corporate, or municipal, depending on the issuer, or short-term, intermediate-term, or long-term, depending on the maturity, investment grade, high-yield, or junk, depending on the bond's quality. Cash may also be classified as money market funds, certificates of deposit, or treasury bills, depending on the kind of instrument or currency. since a result, diversification within asset classes may help you decrease risk while increasing returns, since various subcategories may perform differently in different market situations or occurrences. If you invest in stocks, for example, you may want to diversify across types, such as large-cap, mid-cap, and small-cap, because they may have different growth and volatility potential, or across styles, such as value, growth, and blend. After all, they may have different valuation and performance potential.

Diversify among industries, such as software, biotechnology, or oil and gas, as they may have different competitive and inventive possibilities, or between sectors, such as technology, health care, or energy, as they may have distinct trends and opportunities. Diversify between geographies, such as the United States, Europe, or Asia, because they may have different economic and political potential, or across topics, such as environmental, social, and governance (ESG), because they may have diverse social and ethical potential.

c. Rebalance your portfolio: As we covered in the last chapter, the third strategy to diversify your portfolio is to rebalance your portfolio. Rebalancing may assist you in maintaining your intended risk and return profile while also capitalizing on market fluctuations. Rebalancing is the act of selling assets that have grown more than planned and purchasing investments that have grown less than expected to return your portfolio to its original or target asset allocation. Rebalancing is the practice of purchasing cheap and selling high to maintain the balance of your portfolio.

As a result, by diversifying your portfolio, you may optimize it for your objectives and risk tolerance. This is the common sense approach to investing.

CHAPTER 3: INVESTING STRATEGIES THAT MAKE SENSE

In the last chapter, we looked at common sense investing concepts including investing for the long term, avoiding fees and taxes, and choosing low-cost and tax-efficient solutions. In this chapter, we will learn about common sense investing strategies, which are practical methods and techniques that may help you put the principles into action and achieve your goals.

These methods are based on the best practices and recommendations of some of history's most successful investors, such as Warren Buffett, Benjamin Graham, John Bogle, and Peter Lynch. These strategies are supported by academic research and empirical facts. These strategies are neither difficult nor esoteric, but rather simple and practical. They are the epitome of common sense investing.

Some common sense investing methods are as follows:

1. Arrange your assets: Arranging your assets is the first common sense investing method. This comprises determining how much of your money to invest in different assets, such as stocks, bonds, or cash. The most important decision you can make as an investor is asset allocation, which affects your expected return, risk, and diversification. Asset allocation is also the most personal decision an investor can make since it is determined by their goals, preferences, and circumstances. There is no one-size-fits-all asset allocation approach, however, you may follow certain basic guidelines, such as:

   a. Maintain a balance of risk and return: The core guideline of asset allocation is to maintain a balance of risk and return. This indicates that you should choose an asset allocation strategy that is appropriate for your risk tolerance and projected return. Risk tolerance relates to how much volatility and unpredictability you can endure in your investments. The return expectation is the amount of money you expect to receive from your investments. In general, there is a trade-off between risk and return, which indicates that the greater the reward, the higher the risk, and vice versa. Stocks, for example, generate better returns than bonds but are potentially riskier. As a consequence, choose an asset allocation plan that corresponds to your risk tolerance and predicted return. For example, if you want to make a lot of money and are willing to take on a lot of risk, you should invest more in stocks. If you want poor returns with no risk, you should invest more in bonds or cash.

b. Think about your time horizon: The second asset allocation criterion is to think about your time horizon. This suggests that you should choose an asset allocation strategy that is appropriate for your investment term. The time horizon refers to how long you intend to keep your money invested. In general, the longer your time horizon, the more risky assets, such as stocks, you may invest in, and the shorter your time horizon, the more safe assets, such as bonds or cash, you should invest in. This is because the longer you invest, the more you may benefit from compounding and even out market volatility. If you're saving for retirement and have 30 years to invest, you can afford to take more risks and put more money into stocks. If you just have a year to save for a vacation, you should take less risk and invest more in bonds or cash.

c. Change your asset allocation: The final asset allocation tip is to change your asset allocation. This means that you should review and revise your asset allocation frequently, such as once a year or whenever your goals, preferences, or circumstances change. Your asset allocation may get out of sync with your risk tolerance, expected return, or time horizon for a variety of reasons, including market movements, life events, or personal situations. If the stock market rises, your portfolio may become more stock-heavy than you anticipated, exposing you to more risk than you can bear. Your financial ambitions, expectations, or obligations may change if you marry, have a child, or lose your job, requiring a change in asset allocation. As a consequence, by adjusting your asset allocation, you may keep your portfolio to your objectives and circumstances.

As a consequence, you may optimize your portfolio by distributing your assets depending on your goals and risk tolerance. This is a strategy for investing that is based on common sense.

CHAPTER 4: THE COMMON SENSE OF INVESTING PITFALLS

In the last chapter, we learned about common sense investing methods such as asset allocation, selecting low-cost and tax-efficient investments, and modifying your asset allocation. We will learn about the common sense problems of investing in this chapter, which are the common errors and prejudices that may hurt your investment performance and undermine your objectives.

These traps are based on the observations and cautions of some of history's greatest successful investors, including Warren Buffett, Benjamin Graham, John Bogle, and Peter Lynch. Academic studies and empirical facts back up these dangers. These hazards are not visible or simple to avoid; rather, they are subtle and difficult to resist. They are the adversaries of common sense investment.

The following are some common sense investment pitfalls:

1. Market timing: Market timing is the first fallacy of common sense investment. This implies that you attempt to forecast market moves and purchase or sell appropriately. Market timing is the inverse of long-term investment in that it includes frequent and short-term trading based on projections, trends, or emotions. Market timing is a seductive and popular trap because it plays on your greed and anxiety, as well as your desire to outperform the market and avoid losses. Market timing, on the other hand, is a risky and expensive trap that exposes you to lesser returns, more risk, and higher expenditures. Market timing is a trap for various reasons, including:

   ❖ It is impossible: The first reason market timing is a trap is because it is difficult to achieve. This indicates that you cannot regularly and effectively forecast market movements since they are impacted by a plethora of uncontrollable elements such as supply and demand, news, events, or emotions. The market is complex, dynamic, and efficient, which means that it combines all available information and expectations into its pricing and responds rapidly and surprisingly to new information and expectations. As a result, by the time you act on your forecast, the market may have already moved in the other way or priced it in. For example, if you believe that a favorable economic report would lead the market to rise, the market may have already risen before the report is issued, or it may fall after the report is released due to other causes or expectations. As a result of attempting to time the market, you are more likely to purchase high and sell low, rather than buy cheap and sell high.

❖ It is expensive: The second reason market timing is a trap is because it is expensive. This implies that when you trade more often and for a shorter period, you will have to pay more fees, commissions, and taxes. These expenses may eat into your profits and erode your worth over time. For example, if you put $10,000 in a diversified portfolio that generates 7% interest per year and trade once a year, paying 1% in fees and commissions and 15% in taxes every transaction, you would have $16,367 in ten years, $26,765 in twenty years, and $43,865 in thirty years. However, if you trade once a month and pay the same fees, commissions, and taxes, you will have $12,837 after ten years, $16,481 after twenty years, and $21,166 after thirty years. That's a $22,699 difference, or more than 50% less!

❖ It is unpleasant: The third reason market timing is a bad idea is because it's stressful. As you expose yourself to more changes and emotions, you will have to cope with increased uncertainty and instability. These elements might cause you to worry and anxiety, as well as entice you to make foolish and hasty actions. If you attempt to time the market, for example, you may panic and sell when the market falls, get greedy and purchase when the market rises, or repent and chase when the market swings against your forecast. These practices may cost you money and confidence, as well as chances and rewards.

2. Chasing returns: The second common sense investing trap is chasing returns. This implies that you follow the herd and acquire assets that have lately done well or sell investments that have recently performed badly, without analyzing their fundamentals, value, or prospects. Chasing returns is a common and attractive trap because it appeals to your curiosity and enthusiasm, as well as your desire to join the winners and avoid the losers. Chasing returns, on the other hand, is a risky and expensive trap that exposes you to lesser returns, increased risk, and higher expenses. Chasing returns is a trap for various reasons, including:

> It is illogical: Chasing returns is a trap for many reasons, the first of which is that it is unreasonable. This indicates that you make choices based on emotions like greed, fear, or jealousy rather than rationality like

analysis, assessment, or judgment. Emotions may obscure your mind and distort your vision, causing you to disregard or miss critical facts or circumstances that may affect your investments. For example, if you are looking for high returns, you may purchase an investment that has increased significantly in value without considering its fundamentals, such as profits, growth, or valuation, or its prospects, such as competitive advantage, innovation, or sustainability.

You may also sell an investment that has declined significantly without first investigating its fundamentals, such as assets, cash flow, or dividend, or its prospects, such as turnaround, recovery, or opportunity. As a result, chasing returns leads to the purchase of expensive and overhyped assets and the sale of underpriced and unappreciated opportunities, rather than the purchase of excellent and undervalued investments and the sale of inferior and overpriced investments.

➤ It is ineffective: The second reason why chasing returns is a mistake is because it is ineffective. This indicates you are doing the exact opposite of what you should be doing to attain your objectives and maximize your performance. The primary investing concept is to buy low and sell high, which means to purchase assets when they are cheap and sell them when they are costly. Pursuing returns, on the other hand, causes you to do the opposite: you purchase high and sell low, meaning you acquire assets when they are costly and sell them when they are cheap.

This is because the market is cyclical and mean-reverting, which means that it has ups and downs but tends to return to its average level over time. As a result of chasing profits, you are more likely to acquire assets at their top and sell them at their trough, missing out on the long-term advantages of investing in high-quality, undervalued stocks.

➢ It is expensive: The third reason why chasing returns is a mistake is because it is expensive. This implies that when you trade more often and for a shorter period, you will have to pay more fees, commissions, and taxes. These expenses may eat into your profits and erode your worth over time. For example, if you put $10,000 in a diversified portfolio that generates 7% interest per year and trade once a year, paying 1% in fees and commissions and 15% in taxes every transaction, you would have $16,367 in ten years, $26,765 in twenty years, and $43,865 in thirty years. However, if you trade once a month and pay the same fees, commissions, and taxes, you will have $12,837 after ten years, $16,481 after twenty years, and $21,166 after thirty years. That's a $22,699 difference, or more than 50% less!

3. Overconfidence: The third common sense investment danger is overconfidence. This implies you have an unrealistic and inflated confidence in your talents, expertise, and judgment, and you disregard or discard other people's views, suggestions, or facts. Overconfidence is a trap since it leads to the taking of excessive or needless risks, as well as the disregarding or overlooking of essential facts or circumstances that might damage your investments. Overconfidence is a trap for various reasons, including:

   • It is prejudiced: The first reason overconfidence is dangerous is because it is skewed. This indicates that you are impacted by cognitive and emotional biases such as confirmation bias, hindsight bias, or self-serving bias, which may distort your thinking and perception and cause you to overestimate your abilities while underestimating your faults. For example, if you are overconfident, you may be prone to confirmation bias, which is the propensity to seek, interpret, and recall information that supports your ideas while ignoring, rejecting, or forgetting information that contradicts them. You may also be subject to hindsight bias, which is the propensity to assume that you knew or anticipated the result of an event after it occurred while ignoring or forgetting the event's ambiguity or unpredictability. You may also be subject to self-serving bias, which is the propensity to credit your triumphs to your qualities while attributing your failures to external causes such as chance, the market, or others. As a result of being overconfident, you are more likely to be blind to your flaws and limits, as well as deaf to the comments and criticism of others.

- It is expensive: The second reason why overconfidence is a trap is because it is expensive. This implies you'll have to pay more fees, commissions, and taxes when you trade more often and for a shorter period, based on your ideas rather than facts, data, or study. These expenses may eat into your profits and erode your worth over time. For example, if you put $10,000 in a diversified portfolio that generates 7% interest per year and trade once a year, paying 1% in fees and commissions and 15% in taxes every transaction, you would have $16,367 in ten years, $26,765 in twenty years, and $43,865 in thirty years. However, if you trade once a month and pay the same fees, commissions, and taxes, you will have $12,837 after ten years, $16,481 after twenty years, and $21,166 after thirty years. That's a $22,699 difference, or more than 50% less!

- It is dangerous: The third reason why overconfidence is dangerous is because it is dangerous. This exposes you to additional uncertainty and volatility since you depend on your views rather than facts, statistics, or studies. This might expose you to mistakes, surprises, or shocks that can jeopardize your finances. For example, if you are overconfident, you may invest in a firm that you believe is fantastic without doing enough due diligence, such as analyzing its financial statements, competitive advantage, or development prospects. You may also overlook or disregard warning indicators that suggest difficulties or concerns, such as diminishing wages, mounting debt, or legal issues. You may also neglect to diversify your portfolio, putting all of your eggs in one basket in the hope that it will pay off handsomely. As a result of being overconfident, you are more likely to lose money and confidence, as well as miss out on possibilities and profits.

4. Loss aversion: The fourth common sense investment problem is loss aversion. This implies you prioritize avoiding losses over obtaining gains, and you experience more pain from losing money than pleasure from winning money. Loss aversion is a trap because it may induce you to keep losing assets too long in the hope that they will recover or to sell winning investments too quickly in the fear

that they will decrease. Loss aversion is a trap for various reasons, including:

❖ Irrationality: The first reason loss aversion is a trap is because it is unreasonable. This indicates that you make choices based on emotions like regret, rage, or grief rather than rationality like analysis, assessment, or judgment. Emotions may obscure your mind and distort your vision, causing you to disregard or miss critical facts or circumstances that may affect your investments. For example, if you have loss aversion, you may continue to hang on to a losing investment without assessing its fundamentals, value, prospects, or opportunity cost, which is the value of the next best option that you forego by continuing to hold on to the investment. You may also sell a successful investment without evaluating its fundamentals, value, prospects, or tax consequences, which are the taxes you must pay when you sell the investment. As a result of loss aversion, you are more likely to sell quality and undervalued assets while hanging on to bad and overpriced investments, rather than selling poor and overvalued investments while holding on to quality and undervalued investments.

❖ It is ineffective: The second reason loss aversion is ineffective is because it is ineffective. This indicates you are doing the exact opposite of what you should be doing to attain your objectives and maximize your performance. The fundamental rule of investing is to cut your losses and let your profits run, which means that you should sell your assets when they are below your tolerable loss level and retain them when they are above your projected gain threshold. Loss aversion, on the other hand, causes you to do the opposite: you retain your losses and reduce your gains, which means you maintain your assets while they are below your tolerable loss barrier and sell them when they are over your projected gain threshold. This is because you are terrified of acknowledging your errors and recognizing your losses, or you are afraid of losing your profits and missing out on future opportunities. As a result, if you have loss aversion, you are more likely to lock in your losses and lose out on your gains, reducing your returns and wealth over time.

❖ It is unpleasant: The third reason for loss aversion is because it is stressful. As you expose yourself to more changes and emotions, you will have to cope with increased uncertainty and instability. These elements might cause you to worry and anxiety, as well as entice you to make foolish and hasty actions. For example, if you have loss aversion, you could panic and sell when the market falls, or you might become greedy and purchase when the market rises, or you might repent and chase when the market swings against your expectations. These practices may cost you money and confidence, as well as chances and rewards.

These are the common sense investment traps you should avoid. Investing may be a fun and profitable pastime, but it also demands patience, dedication, and expertise. In the next chapter, we will go over several common sense investing resources that may help you invest intelligently and profitably.

CHAPTER 5: THE COMMON SENSE RESOURCES OF INVESTING

The common sense investing principles, strategies, and pitfalls were covered in the previous chapters. These included investing for the long term, avoiding fees and taxes, selecting high-quality, inexpensive investments, diversifying and rebalancing your portfolio, and avoiding market timing, chasing returns, overconfidence, and loss aversion. We will study common sense investing resources in this chapter. These are trustworthy and practical sources of knowledge and guidance that may assist you in making profitable and sensible investments.

The knowledge and reliability of some of the most reputable and well-respected writers, specialists, and organizations in the investment industry serve as the foundation for these resources. Empirical data and scholarly studies further bolster these resources. These materials are suggestive and chosen rather than comprehensive or definitive.

They embody the core principles of prudent investment.

The resources for investing with common sense are:

1. Books: Books are the primary resource for sensible investment. Books are the most thorough and detailed source of knowledge and guidance on investment since they cover a wide range of subjects, ideas, and methods and provide examples, narratives, and insights. Because they are widely available and reasonably priced, books are also the most accessible and economical source of knowledge and advice on investment. Given that they include the knowledge and expertise of some of the greatest and most successful investors in history, like Warren Buffett, Peter Lynch, John Bogle, and Benjamin Graham, books are also the most enduring and classic source of information and guidance on investing. Thus, you may improve as an investor and learn from the best by reading books.

How do you choose investment books? Here are some pointers:

➢ Look for quality: The first piece of advice when selecting investment books is to consider quality, which is a gauge of a book's accuracy, applicability, and relevance. A book's quality may also be determined by how well-written, structured, and presented it is. A book's quality may also be used to gauge the authority, credibility, and reputation of its publisher, author, or other relevant parties. As a result, you may locate books that are reliable, beneficial, and educational by searching for quality. A book's quality may be determined by several factors, including reviews, ratings, accolades, endorsements, and citations. To determine how a book stands out from the crowd, you may also evaluate its quality against that of its contemporaries, its genre, or its industry. A book on value investing, for instance, might be found by searching for one with a lot of positive reviews, high ratings, prestigious awards, significant endorsements, or citations. One such book is Benjamin Graham's The Intelligent Investor, which is regarded as the bible of value investing and has been endorsed, recommended, and used by many successful investors, including Warren Buffett, who is Graham's most well-known disciple and admirer.

➢ Seek diversity: Seeking variety is a good way to gauge how diversified, comprehensive, and well-balanced a book is when selecting investment books. Another way to gauge how distinctive, original, and unusual a book is is by its variety. Another way to gauge a book's flexibility, adaptability, and applicability is by its variety. Thus, you may locate books that are thorough, engaging, and useful by searching for diversity. A book's diversity may be assessed using several factors, including themes, viewpoints, writing styles, and format types. To observe how a book varies from others, you may also compare its diversity to that of its peers, genre, or area. For instance, if you'd like to read a book on index investing—the strategy of purchasing inexpensive, diversified investments that track an index, like the S&P 500, or a sector, like technology, or a theme, like environmental, social, and governance (ESG)—you can look for one that covers a variety of subjects, like the theory, history, and practice of index investing; or one that presents a variety of viewpoints, like the advantages and disadvantages, the truths and fictions, or the opportunities and challenges of index investing; or one that adopts different formats, like narrative, analytical, or graphical. One such book is The Little Book of Common Sense Investing by John Bogle, which is regarded as the definitive guide in the field.

➢ Seek potential: The third recommendation for investment books is to seek potential, which is a gauge of the amount of worth or advantage a book may provide you. A book's potential may also be used to gauge its potential effect or influence on the reader. The potential may also be used to gauge how much personal development or advancement a book can facilitate. Thus, by searching for potential, you may locate books that have worth, advantages, and influence. A book's potential may be evaluated using a variety of factors, including context, aims, and preferences.

Another way to determine if a book is right for you is to assess how well it aligns with your needs, desires, and expectations. If you want to read a book on growth investing, for instance—which is the strategy of purchasing high-quality, inexpensive investments with room for growth—you can search for one that aligns with your objectives, like learning the fundamentals, becoming an expert in the field, or putting the strategies of growth investing into practice; or one that fits your preferences, like the book's length, writing style, or degree of difficulty; or one that adjusts to your circumstances, like your availability, budget, or ease of access to the book. One Up On Wall Street by Peter Lynch is regarded as one of the best books on growth investing—it's written in a clear, succinct, and humorous manner, it's reasonably priced, and it's widely available.

Thus, you may improve as an investor and learn from the best by reading books. Investing in this manner makes sense.

2. Podcasts: These are the second useful tool for sensible investment. Since you can listen to audio material on your phone, computer, or vehicle at any time, anywhere, podcasts are the most practical and entertaining way to learn about and get advice on investing. Because they cover the most recent news, trends, and changes in the market and let you ask questions, voice your ideas, or provide feedback, podcasts are also the most up-to-date and interactive source of information and advice on

investing. Because they contain a variety of presenters, guests, themes, formats, and styles, podcasts are also the most varied and diversified source of information and advice on investment. You may thus continue to be educated, amused, and active in investing by listening to podcasts.

How can one choose investment podcasts? Here are some pointers:

- seek for quality: As we previously said, the first guideline for selecting investment podcasts is to seek quality. This also applies to selecting investing books. A podcast's quality is determined by its level of accuracy, relevance, and utility. A podcast's quality may also be determined by how well-produced, edited, and presented it is. A podcast's quality may also be determined by how respectable, legitimate, and authoritative its host, guests, or other sources are. As a result, you may discover podcasts that are reliable, beneficial, and educational by searching for quality. A podcast's quality may be evaluated based on several factors, including reviews, ratings, accolades, endorsements, and citations. To determine how a podcast stands out from the crowd, you may also evaluate its caliber its contemporaries, its genre, or its industry. For instance, if you're looking to listen to a podcast about managing your finances, including budgeting, saving, investing, and retiring, you can search for podcasts with a lot of positive feedback, high ratings, awards, recognition, or citations. One such podcast is The Dave Ramsey Show, which is regarded as one of the most well-known and reputable podcasts about personal finance. Its host, Dave Ramsey, is a best-selling author, radio host, and financial expert who has assisted millions of people in becoming debt-free and achieving financial independence.

- Seek variety: As we previously covered, the second recommendation for selecting podcasts on investing is to seek variety. This also applies to selecting books on investment. A podcast's variety reveals how varied, inclusive, and well-rounded it is. Another way to gauge how distinctive, original, and unique a podcast is is by its variety. Another way to gauge a podcast's flexibility, adaptability, and applicability is by its variety. Consequently, you may locate podcasts that are thorough, engaging, and useful by searching for variety. A podcast's diversity may be evaluated based on several factors, including themes, viewpoints, styles, and formats.

To discover how a podcast varies from others, you may also compare its variety to that of its peers, genre, or industry. For instance, if you're interested in listening to a podcast about stock investing—that is, the topic of purchasing and selling company shares—you can search for one that covers a variety of subjects, like the theory, history, and practice of stock investing; or that presents a variety of viewpoints, like the advantages and disadvantages, the facts and myths, or the opportunities and challenges of stock investing; or that employs a variety of approaches, like the persuasive, informative, or entertaining; or that takes on a variety of formats, like the interview, discussion, or monologue. One of the best podcasts on stock investing is The Motley Fool Money, which is hosted by veteran radio host Chris Hill and has featured a host of various guests, including analysts, experts, and CEOs.

- Seek potential: As we previously covered, the third recommendation for selecting investment podcasts is to seek potential. This recommendation also applies to selecting investing books. Potential is a gauge for the amount of value or advantages a podcast can provide you. A podcast's potential may also be used to gauge its potential effect or influence on you. Potential also refers to the amount of development or progress that you can make with the aid of a podcast.

Consequently, you might locate podcasts that are worthwhile, advantageous, and influential by searching for potential. A podcast's potential may be evaluated based on several factors, including aims, interests, and circumstances. Additionally, you may assess how well a podcast suits your requirements, desires, and expectations by contrasting its potential with them.

For instance, if you'd like to listen to a podcast about real estate investing, which is the topic of purchasing and selling real estate, such as homes, apartments, or land, you can search for one that aligns with your objectives, like learning the fundamentals, becoming an expert in the field, or putting the strategies to use, or one that fits your preferences, like the degree of difficulty, the duration, or the podcast's delivery style, or one that adjusts to your circumstances, like your financial constraints, your availability, or your ability to listen to the podcast. One such podcast is the BiggerPockets Real

Estate Podcast, which is regarded as one of the most thorough and useful podcasts on real estate investing, and has been hosted by two successful and experienced real estate investors, David Greene and Brandon Turner.

You may thus continue to be educated, amused, and active in investing by listening to podcasts.

3.   Websites: These are the third resource for sensible investment. Websites provide online material that you can access anytime, anywhere—on your phone, computer, or tablet—making them the most handy and complete source of information and advice on investing. Because they cover the most recent news, trends, and changes in the market and let you ask questions, express your ideas, or provide feedback, websites are also the most up-to-date and interactive source of information and advice on investing. Because websites contain a variety of presenters, guests, themes, genres, and styles, they are also the most diversified and diverse source of information and advice on

investment. You may thus continue to be educated, amused, and interested in investing by browsing websites.

How can one choose investment websites? Here are some pointers:

> Check for quality: As we previously said, the first recommendation for selecting websites for investing is to check for quality. This also applies to selecting books or podcasts about investment. A website's accuracy, relevancy, and usefulness are its key metrics of quality. The degree to which a website is well-designed, well-organized, and well-presented is another indicator of quality. The degree of dependability, authority, and credibility of a website's host, visitor, or source is another indicator of quality. As a result, searching for quality will help you locate reliable, educational, and useful websites. A website's quality may be evaluated based on several factors, including reviews, ratings, accolades, endorsements,

and citations. To understand how a website distinguishes out from the competition, you may also compare its quality to that of its peers, its genre, or its industry. A website on financial news, for instance, might be searched for if it has a lot of positive reviews, high ratings, prestigious awards, significant endorsements, or citations. One such website would be The Wall Street Journal, which is regarded as one of the most reliable and respectable sources of financial news and is published by Dow Jones & Company, a major worldwide provider of news and information services. It features a variety of journalists, experts, or commentators who have been offering insights, analysis, and opinions on the financial world.

➢ Seek variety: As we said before, the second recommendation for websites about investing is to seek diversity. This also applies to the second recommendation for books or podcasts on investment. A website's diversity, scope, and balance are gauged by its variety. Another way to gauge how distinctive, original, and unique a website is is by its variety. Another way to gauge a website's flexibility, adaptability, and applicability is by its variety. Consequently, you might uncover websites that are thorough, engaging, and useful by searching for diversity. A website's diversity may be assessed using several factors, including themes, viewpoints, styles, and forms.

To observe how a website varies from others, you may also compare its diversity to that of its peers, genre, or field. For example, if you want to visit a website on financial education, which is the topic of teaching and learning the skills and knowledge that are necessary to manage your money, such as budgeting, saving, investing, or retiring, you may look for a website that covers various topics, such as the basics, the techniques, or the strategies of financial education, or that offers various perspectives, such as the pros and cons, the myths and facts, or the challenges and opportunities of financial education, or that uses various styles, such as the informative, persuasive, or entertaining, or that adopts various formats, such as the text, video, or audio, such as Khan Academy, which is considered to be one of the most comprehensive and practical websites on financial education, and has been created by Salman Khan, who is an educator and entrepreneur, and has been featuring various instructors, experts, or partners, and has been providing lessons, exercises, and quizzes on various aspects of finance.

➤ Seek potential: As we previously covered, the third recommendation for selecting websites about investing is to seek potential. This recommendation also applies to selecting books or podcasts for investment. Potential is a gauge of the value or advantages a website may provide you.

Potential may also be used to quantify the potential effect or impact that a website may have on you. The potential may also be used to gauge how much development or progress a website can assist with. Consequently, you may locate websites that are significant, helpful, and effective by searching for potential.

A website's potential may be evaluated based on some factors, including aims, interests, and circumstances. You may assess how well a website suits you by contrasting its potential with your requirements, preferences, or expectations. For instance, if you want to visit a website about financial tools—that is, applications or software that can help you manage, track, or optimize your money—for example, budgeting, saving, investing, or retiring—you can search for one that aligns with your objectives, like mastering the features of financial tools or applying their benefits, or one that fits your preferences, like the degree of difficulty, the duration of the website, or the way it is delivered. Or one that adjusts to your circumstances, like your availability, budget, or the website's accessibility, like Mint, which is regarded as one of the most well-liked and helpful websites on financial tools and was created by Intuit, a major provider of financial software and services, and has been featuring various tools, such as budgeting, saving, investing, or retiring, and has been providing guidance, advice, and recommendations on how to manage your money.

4. Courses: These constitute the fourth common sense investing resource. As they provide a curriculum that covers a variety of themes, ideas, and approaches as well as assignments, quizzes, and tests, courses are the most organized and methodical source of knowledge and guidance on investing. As they include lectures, conversations, and comments from instructors, experts, or peers, courses are also the most participatory and entertaining way to learn about investing. Due to

their many levels, methods, and styles, courses are also the most diversified and comprehensive source of knowledge and guidance on investing. You may therefore acquire, practice, and improve your investing knowledge and abilities by enrolling in classes.

How can one choose investing courses? These are some pointers:

- ❖ Look for quality: As we previously said, the first rule for selecting investing books, podcasts, or websites also applies when selecting investing courses. A course's accuracy, relevance, and usefulness are its key metrics of quality. A course's level of organization, delivery, and design may all be measured by its quality. Additionally, quality refers to the authority, credibility, and reputation of the course provider, teacher, or other source. You may thus locate classes that are enlightening, beneficial, and reliable by searching for quality. Numerous factors, including reviews, ratings, accolades, endorsements, and citations, may be used to assess a course's quality. To determine how a course compares to others in its area, genre, or peers, you may also look at its quality in these categories. For instance, if you're interested in taking a course on financial literacy—which is the study of comprehending and putting into practice the knowledge and skills required to manage your finances, such as saving, investing, retirement, or budgeting—you might search for one that has received favorable reviews, high ratings, prominent accolades, influential endorsements, or a lot of citations. One such course is Personal Finance by Coursera, which is regarded as one of the most thorough and useful courses on financial literacy and was developed by the University of Illinois at Urbana-Champaign, a renowned public research university. It has been instructed by a variety of professors, experts, or practitioners and offers lectures, readings, quizzes, and assignments on various aspects of personal finance.

❖ Seek variety: Similar to the previous point about books, podcasts, or websites on investing, the second recommendation for selecting investing courses is to seek diversity. A course's diversity, breadth, and balance are gauged by its variety. A course's degree of originality, distinctiveness, and difference is also gauged by its variety. A further indicator of a course's flexibility, adaptability, and applicability is its variety. Thus, by seeking diversity, you may locate courses that are thorough, engaging, and useful.

Numerous factors, including subjects, viewpoints, methods, or forms, may be used to gauge a course's diversity. A course's diversity may also be compared to that of its peers, genre, or area to determine how unique it is. For example, if you want to take a course on behavioral finance, which is the topic of studying and understanding the psychological and emotional factors that affect the decisions and behaviors of investors, such as biases, heuristics, or emotions, you may look for a course that covers various topics, such as the history, theory, and practice of behavioral finance, or that offers various perspectives, such as the pros and cons, the myths and facts, or the challenges and opportunities of behavioral finance, or that uses various styles, such as the informative, persuasive, or entertaining, or that adopts various formats, such as the online, offline, or hybrid, such as Behavioral Finance by edX, which is considered to be one of the most interesting and innovative courses on behavioral finance, and has been created by the Indian School of Business, which is a premier business school in India, and has been taught by various professors, experts, or practitioners, and has been providing videos, readings, quizzes, and projects on various aspects of behavioral finance.

❖ Seek potential: This is the third recommendation for selecting investing courses. It is also the third recommendation for selecting investing books, podcasts, or websites, as we previously covered. The amount of value or advantage a course can provide you is measured by its potential. The amount of effect or impact a course can have on you is also measured by its potential. Potential also refers to the amount of development or progress that a course may assist you in making. Thus, by searching for potential, you may locate classes that are worthwhile, advantageous, and significant. Numerous factors, including objectives, interests, and circumstances, may be used to gauge a course's potential. One way to determine if a course is right for you is to assess how well its potential matches your requirements, goals, or expectations. For example, if you want to take a course on portfolio management, which is the topic of planning, organizing, and optimizing your investments, such as allocating your assets, choosing your investments, or rebalancing your portfolio, you may look for a course that matches your goals, such as learning the basics, mastering the techniques, or applying the strategies of portfolio management, or that suits your preferences, such as the level of difficulty, the length of time, or the style of delivery of the course, or that adapts to your situation, such as your budget, your availability, or your access to the course, such as Portfolio Management by Udemy, which is considered to be one of the most useful and affordable courses on portfolio management, and has been created by 365 Careers, which is a leading provider of online courses and services, and has been taught by various instructors, experts, or practitioners, and has been providing lectures, exercises, and quizzes on various aspects of portfolio management.

5. Blogs: The fifth resource of common sense investing is blogs. Since blogs include written material that represents the thoughts, experiences, and tales of the bloggers—who are often individual investors, experts, or enthusiasts—they are the most intimate and informal source of knowledge and advice on investing. Because they cover the most recent news, trends, and changes in the market and let you subscribe, share, and comment, blogs are also the most up-to-date and interactive source of information and advice on investing. Because they cover a wide range of subjects, genres, and styles, blogs are also the most diversified and comprehensive source of information and guidance on investing. As a result, reading blogs allows you to interact, learn from, and relate to other investors.

How do you choose investing blogs? Here are a few pointers:

- Look for quality: As we said before, the first rule for selecting investing blogs is the same as the first rule for selecting investing books, podcasts, websites, or courses. A blog's quality is determined by its level of accuracy, relevance, and usefulness. A blog's quality may also be determined by how well-written, well-structured, and well-presented it is. Another way to assess quality is to look at the authority, credibility, and reputation of a blog's writer, platform, or source. As a result, you may locate blogs that are reliable, beneficial, and educational by searching for quality.

A blog's quality may be evaluated based on many factors, including reviews, ratings, accolades, endorsements, and citations. To observe how a blog stands out from the crowd, you may also evaluate its quality against that of its peers, its genre, or its industry. For instance, if you're looking to read a blog about dividend investing, which is the practice of purchasing high-quality, inexpensive investments that pay consistent and growing dividends, you can search for blogs with a lot of citations, awards, and positive reviews. One such blog is Dividend Growth Investor, which is regarded as one of the most reputable and trustworthy blogs on the subject. It is written by DGI, a seasoned and successful dividend investor, and has been offering a variety of articles, analyses, and recommendations on dividend stocks.

- Seek variety: As previously said, the second recommendation for selecting blogs on investing is to seek diversity. This also applies to selecting books, podcasts, websites, or investing courses. Variety is a key indicator of a blog's diversity, scope, and equilibrium. Another way to gauge how distinctive, original, and unique a blog is is by its variety. Another way to gauge a blog's flexibility, adaptability, and applicability is by its variety. Consequently, you may uncover blogs that are thorough, engaging, and useful by searching for diversity. A blog's diversity may be assessed using some factors, including themes, viewpoints, styles, and formats. To understand how a blog stands apart from the rest, you may also compare its variety to that of its peers, genre, or industry. For instance, if you're interested in reading a blog about stock investing, which is the topic of purchasing and selling company shares, you can search for one that addresses a variety of subjects, like the theory, history, and practice of stock investing; or that presents a variety of viewpoints, like the advantages and disadvantages, the truths and myths, or the opportunities and challenges of stock investing; or that employs a variety of styles, like the persuasive, informative, or entertaining; or that uses a variety of media, like text, video, or audio, like The Motley Fool, which is regarded as one of the best blogs on stock investing and was founded by brothers Tom and David Gardner, a multimedia financial services company

- Seek potential: As we previously covered, the third recommendation for selecting blogs about investing is to seek potential. This recommendation is also applicable for selecting books, podcasts, websites, or investing courses. Potential is a gauge for the amount of value or advantages a blog may provide you. A blog's potential may also be used to gauge its potential effect or influence on you. Potential is another way to quantify the amount of development or progress a blog can assist with. You may thus locate blogs that are worthwhile, advantageous, and influential by searching for potential.

A blog's potential may be evaluated based on some factors, including aims, interests, and circumstances. To determine whether blogging is right for you, you may also assess its potential against your requirements, preferences, or expectations. For instance, if you're interested in reading a blog about real estate investing, which is the process of purchasing and selling real estate, such as homes, apartments, or land, you can search for one that aligns with your objectives, like mastering the fundamentals, applying strategies, or finding a blog that fits your preferences, like the degree of difficulty, the length of time, or the blog's writing style, or that adjusts to your circumstances, like your availability, budget, or ease of access to the blog. One such blog is BiggerPockets, which was founded by two successful real estate investors, Joshua Dorkin and Brandon Turner.

6. Videos: These make up the sixth resource for common sense investing. Videos provide audiovisual material that you can view and listen to anytime, anywhere—on your phone, computer, or TV—making them the most active and visually appealing source of knowledge and advice on investing. Because they cover the most recent news, trends, and changes in the market and let you subscribe, share, and discuss, videos are also the most up-to-date and interactive source of information and advice on investing. Because they contain a variety of presenters, guests, themes, genres, and styles, videos are also the most

diversified and diverse source of knowledge and advice on investing. You may thus learn about investing, have fun with it, and become involved by viewing videos.

How do you choose investing videos? Here are a few pointers:

- Seek quality: As we previously said, the first guideline for selecting investing videos is to seek quality. This also applies to selecting books, podcasts, websites, or investing courses. A video's accuracy, relevance, and usefulness are measured by its quality. A video's quality may also be determined by how well-produced, edited, and distributed it is. A video's quality may also be determined by how reliable, trustworthy, and authoritative its presenter, guest, or source is. As a result, you may locate films that are reliable, beneficial, and educational by searching for quality. A video's quality may be determined by several factors, including reviews, ratings, accolades, endorsements, and citations. To understand how a video stands out from the crowd, you may also assess its quality by comparing it to that of its peers, its genre, or its industry. For instance, if you want to watch a video on financial planning, which is the subject of setting and achieving your financial goals, such as saving, investing, or retiring, you may look for a video that has positive reviews, high ratings, prestigious awards, influential endorsements, or numerous citations, such as How to Retire Early: The Shockingly Simple Math by TEDx Talks, which is considered to be one of the most inspirational and practical videos on financial planning, and has been presented by Mr.

- Seek variety: As we said before, the second advice for selecting investing videos is to seek diversity, much as the second suggestion for selecting investing books, podcasts, websites, or courses. The amount of diversity, breadth, and balance in a video is determined by its variety. Another way to gauge how distinctive, creative, and unique a video is is by its variety. Variety also serves as a gauge for a video's adaptability, flexibility, and usefulness. You may thus uncover films that are thorough, engaging, and useful by searching for variety. A video's diversity may be assessed using several factors, including themes, viewpoints, styles, and formats. To observe how a video varies from others, you may also compare its diversity to that of its peers, genre, or industry.

For instance, if you're interested in watching a video on stock analysis—that is, the process of assessing and choosing stocks based on their fundamentals, like earnings, growth, cash flow, assets, or dividends—you can search for one that addresses a variety of subjects, like the theory, history, and practice of stock analysis; or that presents a range of viewpoints, like the advantages and disadvantages, the truths and fictions, or the opportunities and challenges of stock analysis; or that employs a variety of forms, like the lecture, demonstration, or case study One of the most thorough and useful videos on stock analysis is How to Value a Stock - Picking the Best Valuation Method for Each Company by Learn to Invest. Jimmy, an investor and educator, created the video and has been teaching different methods like discounted cash flow, dividend discount, or price multiples and has demonstrated how to apply them to various companies like Apple, Coca-Cola, or Netflix.

- Seek potential: As we previously covered, the third recommendation for selecting investing videos is the same as the third recommendation for selecting investing books, podcasts, websites, or courses. Potential is a gauge for the amount of value or advantage a video can provide you. A video's potential may also be used to gauge its potential effect or influence on you. The potential may also be used to gauge how much personal development or advancement a video can assist with. You may thus locate films that are worthwhile, advantageous, and influential by searching for potential. A video's potential may be assessed using some factors, including situational factors, aims, and personal preferences. You may assess how well a film suits you by contrasting its potential with your requirements, preferences, or expectations.

For instance, if you'd like to watch a video on passive income—that is, the topic of making money without having to work for it—you can search for one that aligns with your objectives, like learning the fundamentals, becoming an expert in the field, or putting the strategies into practice—or that meets your preferences, like the video's length, difficulty level, or delivery style—or that adjusts to your circumstances, like your financial constraints, your availability, or your ability to watch the video. How to Make Money

Online by Practical Wisdom: 10 Trusted Ways to Earn Money and Passive Income Online One of the most helpful and reasonably priced videos about passive income is Interesting Ideas, which was made by Practical Wisdom, a YouTube channel that offers tips and ideas on how to make money and better your life. It has featured a variety of methods, like e-commerce, podcasting, and blogging, and it has been offering direction, advice, and suggestions on how to generate money online.

6. Forums: Common sense investing's sixth resource is forums. Because they provide online venues where you may engage with other investors, professionals, or enthusiasts and discuss ideas, views, or experiences, forums are the most social and community source of knowledge and advice on investing. Because they cover the most recent news, trends, and changes in the market and let you submit questions, comments, and answers, forums are also the most up-to-date and interactive source of information and advice on investing.

Because they cover a wide range of subjects, genres, and styles, forums are also the most diversified and comprehensive source of information and guidance on investing. As a result, you may interact, learn from, and relate to other investors by joining forums.

How can one choose investing forums? Here are a few pointers:

- Quality search: Just as we previously said, the first advice for selecting books, podcasts, websites, courses, or films on investing is to search for quality when selecting forums. A forum's quality is determined by its level of accuracy, relevance, and usefulness. Additionally, a forum's quality may be determined by how well-moderated, well-organized, and well-presented it is. A forum's quality is also determined by how respectable, legitimate, and authoritative its administrators, moderators, and members are. As a result, you may locate forums that are reliable, beneficial, and educational by searching for quality. A forum's quality may be evaluated based on several factors, including reviews, ratings, accolades, endorsements, and citations. To determine how a forum stands out from the others, you may also evaluate its quality about that of its peers, genre, or industry. If you'd like to join a forum on value investing, for instance—value investing is the strategy of purchasing high-quality, inexpensive investments—you could search for one with a lot of positive feedback, awards, recognition, or citations.

One such forum is Value Investors Club, which is regarded as one of the most reputable and trustworthy on the subject and was founded by renowned value investor and author Joel Greenblatt. It has several members, moderators, and administrators who are all successful and experienced value investors and has been offering a variety of posts, analyses, and recommendations on value stocks.

- Seek variety: Similar to the previous suggestion about books, podcasts, websites, courses, or videos, the second recommendation for selecting investing forums is to seek variety. Variety is a key indicator of a forum's degree of diversity, breadth, and balance. Another way to gauge how distinctive, innovative, and diverse a forum is is by its variety. A forum's degree of flexibility, adaptability, and applicability may also be gauged by its variety. Thus, you may uncover forums that are thorough, engaging, and useful by searching for diversity.

A forum's diversity may be assessed using some factors, including themes, viewpoints, forms, and styles. To evaluate how a forum varies from others, you may also compare its diversity to that of its peers, genre, or field. For example, if you want to join a forum on index investing, which is the strategy of buying low-cost and diversified investments that track an index, such as the S&P 500, or a sector, such as technology, or a theme, such as environmental, social, and governance (ESG), you may look for a forum that covers various topics, such as the history, theory, and practice of index investing, or that offers various perspectives, such as the pros and cons, the myths and facts, or the challenges and opportunities of index investing, or that uses various styles, such as the informative, persuasive, or entertaining, or that adopts various formats, such as the thread, comment, or poll, such as Bogleheads, which is considered to be one of the best forums on index investing, and has been inspired by John Bogle, who is the founder of Vanguard and the pioneer of index investing, and has been featuring various members, moderators, or administrators, who are all fans and followers of Bogle and his philosophy, and has been providing various posts, discussions, and votes on index investing.

- Seek potential: This is the third recommendation for selecting investing forums, and it is also the third recommendation for selecting investing books, podcasts, blogs, courses, or videos, as we previously covered. Potential is a gauge for the amount of value or advantages a forum may provide you. Potential also refers to the extent to which a forum may affect or influence you. Potential may also be used to gauge the extent to which a forum can assist you in developing or improving. You may thus choose forums that are worthwhile, advantageous, and significant by searching for potential.

A forum's potential may be evaluated based on some factors, including circumstances, aims, and preferences. A forum's potential might be compared to your requirements, preferences, or expectations to see if it is a good match for you. For instance, if you'd like to join a forum on cryptocurrency investing—that is, the topic of buying and selling digital currencies like Dogecoin, Ethereum, or Bitcoin—you can search for one that aligns with your objectives, like learning the fundamentals, becoming an expert in the field, or putting the strategies to use. You can also search for a forum that fits your preferences, like the degree of difficulty, the duration of the discussion, or the forum's communication style, or one that adjusts to your circumstances, like your availability, your budget, or your budget, like Reddit, which is regarded as one of the most well-known and active forums on cryptocurrency investing.

As a result, you may interact, learn from, and relate to other investors by joining forums.

CHAPTER 6: CONCLUSION

Congratulations! This is the last page of the book. You now know the basics of investing and how to use common sense. You now know how to steer clear of the common sense mistakes made while investing. You now know where to look for and how to employ common sense resources while investing. You are now proficient at using common sense while investing.

Your adventure with investing does not finish here, however. This is just the start. Investing is a continuous process of growth, learning, and adaptation. Investing isn't something you do once and then forget about. Your objectives, tastes, and circumstances are subject to change, so you must periodically assess and modify your investments. As the investing environment changes and new possibilities and concerns present themselves, you must remain knowledgeable and aware.

As a result, I urge you to continue developing as an investor. I urge you to read more investing-related books, articles, and blogs. I urge you to tune in to further investing-related podcasts, seminars, and interviews. I urge you to get involved in additional investing-related communities, forums, and organizations. Others may gain from your ideas and criticism, thus I strongly advise you to share your expertise.

Recall that investing is about more than simply money. It concerns your life. It concerns your ideals, aspirations, and ambitions. It concerns your community, friends, and family. It concerns your contribution, influence, and legacy. Investing is not a goal unto itself; it is a means to an end. You may use investing as a tool to realize your dream of living a contented and joyful life.

I thus hope your investing endeavors are filled with success. I hope you have all you deserve—happiness, prosperity, and contentment. May your life be filled with plenty, significance, and direction. I appreciate you taking the time to read. With common sense, let's keep investing.